The Unseen, the Unsightly and the Amusing in Sheffield

J. EDWARD VICKERS

By the same author:

J. EDWARD VICKERS

The Unseen the Unsightly and the Amusing

IN SHEFFIELD

The **Hallamshire** Press 1997

© The Hallamshire Press 1997

Published by The Hallamshire Press
The Hallamshire Press is an Imprint of
Interleaf Productions Limited
Broom Hall
8–10 Broomhall Road
Sheffield S10 2DR
England

Typeset by Interleaf Productions Limited
Printed in Spain by Edelvives

British Library Cataloguing in Publication Data
    Vickers, J. Edward (John Edward) , 1917-
        The unseen, the unsightly and the amusing in Sheffield
        1.Sheffield (England) - History
        I.Title
        942.8'21

    ISBN 1 874718 36 9

About the Author

J. Edward Vickers was a tutor of Sheffield History for Adult Education until retirement. He is a member of the Society of Architectural Historians of Great Britain and of the Hunter Archaeological Society. As a founder member and Vice-President of the Hallamshire Historic Buildings Society, he has assisted in the saving of many of the historic buildings of the city.

He was born in 1917 and studied art and architecture at the Sheffield School of Art. Enlisting with the Hallamshire Battalion of the Territorial Army in 1938, he was called to the colours immediately the Second World War began. He served throughout the war, seeing service in Norway, Iceland, North Africa, Italy and Austria. He married his wife Ruby in 1941 and they have three sons and a granddaughter.

For his work on the history of Sheffield and the conservation of many of its buildings, he was awarded the M.B.E. by the Queen in 1994.

Illustrations

All the illustrations in this book are from photographs taken by the author, with the exception of certain old photographs and drawings which are from the author's collection.

Greatly enlarged with new features, photographs and anecdotes, this book is based on *The Odd, Amusing and Unusual in Sheffield*, compiled and published by J. Edward Vickers in 1986.

Author's Note

I FIND IT amazing that most Sheffield people, many working in or passing through the centre of the city every weekday, fail to see the interesting things that surround them. In fact, most people's eyes tend to rest on the shop windows, even though there is little difference between one store's windows and the next!

Yet the buildings above these windows have many facets of interest, quite apart from their architectural revulsion or delight. These things, carvings, plaques, statues, etc., I call 'Not exactly hidden—but unseen'.

In addition, anyone caring to take a leisurely walk around our city and suburbs will find all kind of odd and interesting things, especially in our churchyards and parks. They will also see much that is unsightly and some examples of these are included in the following pages.

For amusement and knowledge of Sheffield's history I have given many anecdotes and stories, all of which, I can assure the reader, are perfectly true!

I hope the photographs, with my comments and stories, will bring enlightenment, together with many a smile, or a tear, to the reader and that he or she will look with more interest in the future on our fair city.

'The time has come,' the historian said,
'To talk of many things,
Of trees and tombs and troubled times,
of carvings and of kings!'

With apologies to Lewis Carroll

To my wife Ruby
with thanks for all the
help and assistance in the
compilation of this book.

THE UNSEEN,
THE UNSIGHTLY
AND THE AMUSING

THE FATE OF SHEFFIELD'S MEMORIALS

IN THE Cholera Gardens on Norfolk Road is a broken monument to the people who died during the terrible cholera epidemic in 1832. The dreaded disease made its appearance in England in 1831 and gradually spread across the country.

It appeared in Sheffield in the July of the following year and 1,347 people were attacked by the epidemic. The main causes were the terrible sanitary conditions and open drains, so prevalent in England at that time.

In Sheffield, 402 of the townsfolk died, one of them being the Master Cutler, John Blake. A large proportion of the victims were buried in mass graves in the Cholera Gardens, but there is a gravestone for the important cutler, John Blake.

The large pointed monument was broken in a gale some years ago, but the base still stands. The upper part of this fine monument is being kept in the Council's Works Depot at Olive Grove, from where it will be replaced at some future date.

The grave of John Blake, Master Cutler

The Cholera Monument in 1986

The broken monument in 1996

THE CRIMEAN WAR MEMORIAL

THE Crimean War Memorial formerly stood at Moorhead. Placed there by subscription, Florence Nightingale being one of the subscribers, the monument commemorated the soldiers and sailors killed in that war of 1854–56.

It was dismantled and moved to the Botanical Gardens in 1960. Under the memorial was found a copper plate recording the names of the architect and the builders. Inside a glass jar near the plate were newspapers of 1857, silver coins of the value of one penny, half penny, farthing and half farthing.

Unfortunately the fine pillar on which the statue of Victory was seated was not re-erected when the memorial was taken to the Botanical Gardens. Instead Victory sits on the base stone and the pillar was broken into a number of pieces and is now on a children's playground in Hammond Street!

THE QUEEN'S OBELISK

THE Queen's Obelisk was erected in honour of Victoria's Jubilee in 1887, and was situated in the centre of the Town Hall Square. It was moved from there in 1905 to make way for the Queen Victoria statue.

The Jubilee Obelisk was then re-erected in Endcliffe Park, where it stands now.

The author was walking through the park a few years ago when he noticed a man with a child looking at the Obelisk. Clutching his father's sleeve the little boy asked, 'What's that, Dad?' The man thought for a second or two, then scratched his head. 'I think its Cleopatra's Needle, son,' he said.

The statue of Queen Victoria that took over the site of the Jubilee Obelisk, has now been relegated to Endcliffe Park. At each side of the base stone on which the Queen sits, are other figures. On one side is a strong muscular man holding a large hammer. He represents 'Labour'. On the opposite side is the figure of a woman, with a baby at her breast and a young girl standing at their side. This group represents 'Maternity'. It has been suggested by a number of people that the lady should really represent 'Conservative', thus satisfying both political parties!

Figures representing 'Labour' (left) and 'Maternity' (right) on the base of the Victoria Obelisk

The-Unseen the Unsightly and the Amusing in Sheffield

Queen Victoria's Obelisk in Endcliffe Park

The Queen Victoria Monument in Endcliffe Park

CARVINGS GALORE

ONE OF Sheffield's most interesting buildings is the Town Hall, built in 1896 and opened by Queen Victoria the following year.

The main front in Pinstone Street has a frieze of the same width as the one on the Parthenon at Athens. On the left side of the doorway, preceded by the 'Goddess of Light', there are portrayed the most skilled of the arts and crafts, such as architects, painters, workers in precious metals, etc. Preceded by the 'Goddess of Plenty', on the right hand side, are smiths, smelters, miners, etc. Also our famous bulldog!

Above the front arch are the arms of Sheffield, supported by the gods Thor and Vulcan, whilst above this is the statue of Queen Victoria. At the summit of the clock tower, 210 feet high, is the nude statue of Vulcan, the god of Fire and Metal Workers. The model for Vulcan was one of Queen Victoria's Life Guardsmen. This statue weighs eighteen hundredweight and is seven feet in height.

Other sculptural decorations on the Surrey Street side are two figures, one representing 'Peace' and the other 'War'.

The most curious decorations are situated above two windows, high on the corner of the 1923 extensions in Surrey Street. These are stone carvings of an owl and a pelican.

According to the official guide book issued after the extensions were opened, 'These birds are there to represent the wisdom and intelligence of the City Council'.

The Town Hall

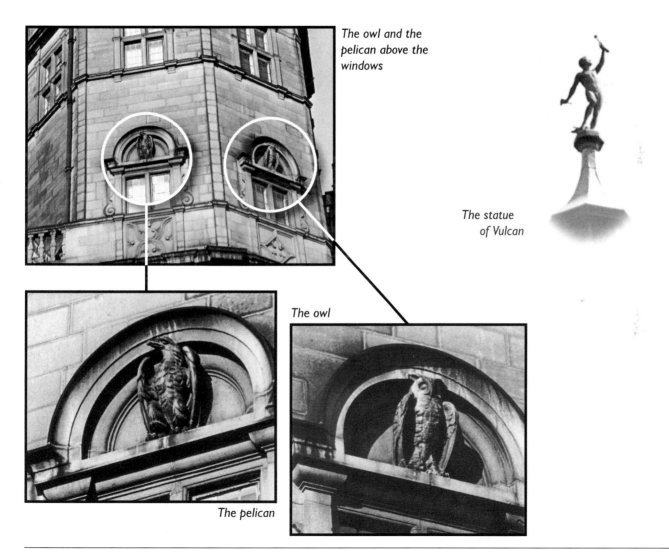

The owl and the pelican above the windows

The statue of Vulcan

The owl

The pelican

31967. Sheffield, St Paul's Church. F.F & Cº

THE SCATTERED ODDMENTS OF A CHURCH

THE ONCE BEAUTIFUL Peace Gardens, situated in front of the latest extensions to the Town Hall, were originally the site of a fine church called St Paul's.

The foundation stone of the church was laid in 1720, but because of a quarrel about the right of presentation, the church was not opened until 1740, twenty years after the commencement of the building. A large dome was added in 1769, making St Paul's one of the finest churches in the town.

Unfortunately it was demolished in 1938 and ornaments and oddments were taken from the building to various parts of the city. Some of the main pieces were transferred to a smaller church of the same name which was built at Arbourthorne in the suburbs, but this church also has now been demolished. A number of the stone decorations that surrounded the dome of the original St Paul's can now be seen at Bents Green used as garden ornaments. Also an unusual frieze, part of the old church, can be seen on a house in Trap Lane.

Oddment from St Paul's Church, now in Trap Lane

Oddment from St Paul's Church at Bents Green

*The-**Unseen** the **Unsightly** and the **Amusing** in **Sheffield***

THE BEASTS OF FARGATE

IN FARGATE in the centre of Sheffield, on the finely restored facade of the premises of W.H. Smith, are carved stone heads of pigs and cows. These may appear incongruous considering the building is a very large newsagents and bookstore.

However, the original use of the premises, erected in 1882, was for Arthur Davy and Sons Ltd, pork butchers and provision merchants.

For many years the ground floor was a provision shop, whilst the remainder of the building was adapted for use as a cafe-restaurant.

The pig

The cow

THE GREAT STORM OF 1729

BETWEEN FIVE and six o'clock in the morning it began to thunder, lighten and rain in the most violent manner and this continued without a break until two o'clock in the afternoon. The storm caused all the rivers to flood and a great deal of damage was done.

The River Sheaf overflowed its banks and flooded the Shrewsbury Hospital, causing one end to be washed away.

The Chapel, situated in the centre of the hospital, was filled with sludge and all its furniture was lost. One old man and a woman, together with four horses from the stables, were drowned in the flood.

MORE UNUSUAL WEATHER

THE YEAR 1911 was remarkable for the very high temperatures recorded. In June there were three weeks of hot weather, with a temperature on the 8th of 80°F. On the 6th July the temperature rose to 82°, on the 21st it was 86° and on the 28th 87°. In August it was 85° on the 8th, but on the following day it reached 92°, the highest ever known in Sheffield!

September continued to be hot, with 87°F on the 8th. The rainfall for January to August was only 13.57 inches, as against an average of 22.08 inches. In July only 0.21 inches fell against an average of 2.81 inches.

The following year, 1912, restored the balance. It was the wettest and coldest ever remembered! Only two sunny days were experienced during the whole year!

THE CRAFTSMEN OF SHEFFIELD

PROMINENT IN Fitzalan Square are the 'White Buildings', constructed in 1908 by architects Flockton and Gibbs. Local craftsmen, the Tory Brothers, architectural and monumental sculptors, of Ecclesall Road, carved the figures representing Sheffield trades. They show a hand grinder, file cutter, crucible steel making and silver chasing.

The file cutter, etc.

Crucible steel making, etc.

The Unseen the Unsightly and the Amusing in Sheffield

FITZALAN SQUARE

FITZALAN SQUARE is notable for having the only monument still in its original site. This is the King Edward VII statue, which stands on a pedestal in the centre of the square. The king faces High Street and his head and shoulders always seem to make a perfect perch for our Sheffield pigeons.

At the corner of the square and High Street, is a new building on the site of the Marples Hotel. The Marples, a seven-storey hotel, received a direct hit from a German bomber during the Second World War. The heavy high-explosive bomb was dropped in the terrible raid on Sheffield of 12th December, 1940. The premises were completely destroyed, the whole building collapsing on the many people who were sheltering inside. Between sixty and seventy people were killed, many of them women.

Statue of King Edward VII

GRAFFITI

UNFORTU- NATELY Sheffield, like so many of the large cities in Britain, suffers from uncaring people who think it is clever to cover build- ings with brightly coloured graffiti. The photograph shows a doorway in Fitzalan Square, only a few feet away from the King Edward memorial!

Graffiti-covered doorway in Fitzalan Square

The Unseen the Unsightly and the Amusing in Sheffield

An Old Children's Shelter

AT THE CORNER of Surrey Street and Norfolk Street, on a building now belonging to the Halifax Building Society, is preserved a doorway which originally led to the 'Jeffie Bainbridge Children's Shelter'.

Jeffie was the wife of Emerson Bainbridge who, in addition to being a Justice of the Peace, was a mining engineer and a well-known philanthropist. It was he who provided the money to build the large Y.M.C.A. building in Fargate. (The Y.M.C.A. vacated these premises for more modern buildings in Broomhall).

When Jeffie died, her husband erected the Children's Shelter as a memorial to her and this was opened by the Duchess of Portland in December, 1894.

The object of the home was to provide shelter and food for the waifs and strays of the town. For many years afterwards any poor, barefoot and hungry child, of which there were many at that time, could be sure of a bowl of soup and accommodation for the night.

The Halifax Building Society are to be commended for preserving the doorway, an interesting insight into Sheffield's past.

Doorway to the Shelter

CLEANLINESS IS NEXT TO GODLINESS

IN THE WICKER in 1780 a bathing house owned by Joseph Rowbotham was situated opposite the **Nursery** (later to become **Nursery Street**).

Bathing dresses were supplied at a charge of one penny per person and the River Don ran through the baths to ensure fresh, clean water!

 DROWNING IN THE RIVER SHEAF

ON SUNDAY 29th March, 1812, a party from Mount Pleasant, which included Samuel Broomhead Ward, his wife, two sons, three daughters and a nursemaid, were out walking in the fields nearby. The family had to cross a none-too-safe wooden bridge that spanned the Sheaf, which was a rushing torrent due to previous heavy rainfall. All but the nurse and two-year-old Anne Ward got safely over. Just as these two stepped on to the rickety old bridge, it collapsed and they were both thrown into the water.

With some difficulty the nurse was rescued, but the little girl had disappeared under the water and was later pulled out dead.

Normally the River Sheaf is only three to four inches deep!

 CURIOUS INSCRIPTION

IT APPEARS to have been the custom for all of the old Medical Schools to have the Latin inscription 'Ars Longa Vita Brevis' carved in stone over their main doorway. This inscription can still be seen on the old Medical School in Sheffield, now the Bank of Scotland, in Leopold Street.

A larger version of the Latin inscription that existed on a building (now demolished) in Surrey Street, has been preserved and is now fitted on to a wall on the south-west side of the large modern Hallamshire Hospital.

It is probably a good thing that most patients entering the hospital cannot understand Latin, for translated the inscription reads, 'Art is long, Life is short'.

A curious inscription

Plaque— Hallamshire Hospital

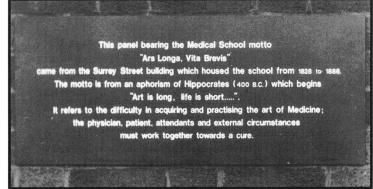

This panel bearing the Medical School motto
"Ars Longa, Vita Brevis"
came from the Surrey Street building which housed the school from 1828 to 1888.
The motto is from an aphorism of Hippocrates (400 B.C.) which begins
"Art is long, life is short.....".
It refers to the difficulty in acquiring and practising the art of Medicine;
the physician, patient, attendants and external circumstances
must work together towards a cure.

Two Very Odd Notices

IN THE GROUNDS of the Sheffield Royal Infirmary, now closed, a notice used to state, 'Guard Dogs Operate Here'.

However, the most amusing was a large sign over a 'junk shop' at the Highfield end of Abbeydale Road, which stated very clearly, 'Antiques—Old and New'!

How History Repeats Itself

A NEWS ITEM of 14th March, 1885, reported that: 'Repeated burglaries, in the Heeley and Nether Edge districts are causing great alarm to householders'.

Later, on 22nd June, of the same year, the Salvation Army, with General Booth present, met in the Albert Hall, Barker's Pool, to: 'protest against the present state of the law and the immorality of the times'.

Suicide or Murder?

ON THE 11th October, 1885, the body of John Heald, bell-ringer and peace-keeper at the Parish Church (now the Cathedral), was discovered in the canal at Attercliffe!

A VERY ODD NOTICE

AT THE TOP of Norfolk Street is the Upper Chapel. This fine brick building with its stone facade was built in 1700, but took on its present appearance in 1848.

Some years ago on the 'wayside pulpit' was a message reading: 'Be kind—we are all god's creatures'.

The curious and amusing thing about this notice was that, just opposite, nailed to a tree, a signboard stated: 'Don't Feed the Pigeons—Offenders will be Prosecuted'.

'Don't Feed the Pigeons'—with wayside pulpit in the background

The Mortality of the Young

IN THE GRAVEYARD of the Upper Chapel are a number of poignant reminders of the bad old days when there was a very high mortality rate amongst the young. An inscription on one gravestone demonstrates this sad fact most clearly:

In memory of Henry, son of Edward and Jane Jones, died 20th September, 1828, aged 3 years.

Also son Edward, died 4th June, 1832, aged 8 months.

Also daughter Ann, died 1st January, 1840, aged 1 year and 5 months.

Also daughter Jane, died 2nd October, 1846, aged 16 years.

Also daughter Sarah, died 4th June, 1849, aged 20 years.

Also son Edward, died 16th April, 1853, aged 3 years.

Sheffield's First Certified Pilot

BORN IN 1893, Marcus Manton was the son of a prominent surgeon living at Norfolk Park. After leaving school he studied engineering until he was old enough to take his pilot's certificate. Then in 1912, against the wishes of his father and family, he left the city to join the Grahame-White School of Flying at Hendon, just outside London.

Still only 18 years old, Manton gained his pilot's certificate, becoming one of the youngest men in the country to do so. He was immediately employed as an instructor at the school.

An Unusual Statue

ON CAIRNS' BUILDINGS in Church Street, is the statue of a man unknown to most Sheffield people. Standing in a niche under a canopy the sculpture is of Hugh McCalmont, the Earl of Cairns.

Cairns, one of the now forgotten eminent Victorians, was born at Cultra, County Down, on December 27th, 1819, and was called to the English Bar in 1844. He entered Parliament in 1852 as member for Belfast, was appointed Solicitor-General in 1858, and in 1866, when Lord Derby returned to office, he was made Attorney-General. When Disraeli took office in 1868, he offered him the Lord Chancellorship. Cairns died at Bournemouth on April 2nd, 1885.

Cairns Buildings, or Chambers, was built in 1895, the architect being Charles Hadfield. The building was badly damaged during the Sheffield Blitz in 1940, but most of the front remained unscathed.

Lord Cairns, with his air of judicial calm, still continues to preside impassively over the proceedings in Church Street, as impervious to passers-by as they are to him.

The statue of Lord Cairns on Cairns' Chambers, Church Street

HOUSE WITH A COAT OF ARMS

BUILT BY the Duke of Norfolk, just over a hundred years ago, this fine house on Burngreave Road has, over the doorway, the old Sheffield Coat of Arms.

Many local people call it the Police Station, for the Sheffield police had it on lease for 97 years, and it was probably the home of the Chief Superintendent. Today the house is numbered 24, but it was probably the first house to be built on the new Burngreave Road. All the other houses, built after this one, were the homes of very wealthy Sheffield businessmen and merchants.

How Much Proof Did He Want?

AT THE Sheffield court on the 19th January, 1903, the Magistrate refused to declare a woman a habitual drunkard, even though she had been convicted 86 times in total, 10 times in the last year. He said there was not sufficient evidence to show that she couldn't take care of herself!

A Policeman's Lot is Not a Happy One

IN 1926 when Captain P.J. Sillitoe was Chief Constable, he made his first annual report to the City Council. This was said by the Chairman to be the first report of a Sheffield Chief Constable for 40 years!

    The report contained quite a number of recommendations which led to one member of the Council enquiring whether Sheffield was about to come under a military dictatorship.

Would They Do It Today?

IN THE 1870s the firm of Osborne's was in a difficult position with regard to finance. To save the firm, all the workmen at Osborne's Tower Wheel in Blonk Street worked for one week for no wages!

A Grand 21st Birthday

AT THE coming of age of James Dixon of Stumperlowe Hall, all the work people of Dixon's firm assembled at Ranmoor at 10 o'clock in the morning and, headed by the Hallamshire Rifles Band, marched in a grand procession to the hall. Later they were divided into five groups, each group being feasted and entertained at an hotel or inn.

A Curious Head

IN STAVELEY ROAD, just off Abbeydale Road, on a row of modern houses is a curious head. This carving in stone was originally on a block of old houses that stood on the same site.

This most aristocratic-looking face persuaded people living around that it was an effigy of 'Lord Staveley' and for many years it was the custom for men passing under the figurehead to lift their hats in respect to the old gentleman.

Unfortunately, there is no record of a Lord Staveley ever having existed!

The old houses in Staveley Road were demolished in 1978, but the remarkable head was preserved by the City Council and was later attached to the newly built block of homes.

N ODD FACE

AN ODD face-carving was formerly situated on the corner of an old barn at Jordanthorpe Hall Farm, Norton.

This very crude carving of a face is considered to be of Norman origin, for most of the stones for this barn came from Beauchief Abbey which was built in 1183 and demolished in 1537. Unfortunately the barn, together with many other ancient buildings, was demolished to make way for the by-pass road, Bochum Parkway.

 LONG HARD PULL

IN THE Heeley Churchyard is a large obelisk to the memory of John Shortridge, of Chipping House, Abbeydale. He was the builder of the railway from Sheffield to Manchester and was also responsible for the erection of the massive Wicker Arches.

The immense block of granite on which the obelisk stands took 20 horses to draw it up the hill to the churchyard.

 BRONTË CONNECTION

NEAR THE chancel of Heeley Church is a memorial stone to Thomas Wooler, a surgeon, formerly of Dewsbury, who died in 1895, at the age of 92.

For several years he lived in retirement at Heeley. He was the brother of Margaret Wooler, friend and schoolmistress of Charlotte Brontë. Thomas Wooler was a personal friend of the Brontë family.

A FORGOTTEN COMPOSER

STERNDALE BENNETT was the third and only son of Robert Bennett, a native of Ashford-in-the-Water. He was born on April 13th, 1816, at No. 7 Howard Street, which stood in a block of property demolished in the 1960's to make way for Arundel Gate. After his father's death, the young Bennett went to live with his maternal parents at Cambridge and there he entered the Royal Academy of Music as a boarder shortly before his tenth birthday.

He wrote his first piano concerto, which was greatly praised by Mendelssohn, at the age of 16. This was only the first of many compositions which were well received. Later in life he founded the Bach Society, which introduced the great choral works of J.S.B. to this country. He then became principal of the academy and professor of music at Cambridge University and was knighted in 1871.

Today he is commemorated by a plaque fixed to the wall of Novotel, Arundel Gate. Formerly a plaque was fixed to a large stone nearby marking the place where stood the cottage in which he was born.

Plaque to Sterndale Bennett

Terrorist Tactics

IN NOVEMBER 1839, during the Chartists Risings, an attempt was made to demolish St Mary's Church in Bramall Lane, by the throwing of fire bombs.

Luckily the plot failed, as, upon throwing, most of the fuses became detached from the crudely made bombs!

The leader of the terrorists, Samuel Holberry, died in prison in 1842. As their plans were to take over the Town Hall and kill anyone who opposed them, it seems rather strange that a plaque to Samuel Holberry is now affixed to the Town Hall extensions!

Plaque to Samuel Holberry

GOD BLESS THE DUKES

AN UNUSUAL inscription could have been seen a short time ago on a lodge situated at the lower entrance to Norfolk Park. Carved on the wooden porch were the words 'God Bless the Queen and the Howards—1857'.

The Queen was the famous Victoria who ruled over Britain and its empire for over 60 years. The Howards are the Dukes of Norfolk and it was the present Duke of Norfolk's uncle who presented the park to the city of Sheffield in 1909.

Unfortunately all our parks and their buildings have been sadly neglected over the last few years and this formerly beautiful lodge was taken over by squatters and vandalised. As can be seen in the last photograph on page 51, the porch is ruined, all windows are broken, there are holes in the roof and graffiti all over the building.

An unusual inscription

PANIC IN CHURCH

WHEN THE Ebenezer Chapel at Shalesmoor was opened in July 1823, someone noticed a crack in the ceiling plaster. Shouting that the place was falling down, the man caused a packed congregation to panic and in the confusion, in addition to the damage caused to the church fittings, 700 panes of glass were broken!

A WONDERFUL OLD WOMAN

MRS AUSTIN was only a small lady, about 4 feet in height and weighing between 4 and 5 stones.

Though born in Scotland, she lived most of her life in Sheffield. She was the widow of a sea captain and she died in this city in May, 1872, at the age of 97.

After the death of her husband, who was lost at sea, she earned her living by knitting and then hawking her handicrafts around the country.

She thought nothing of walking from Sheffield to Manchester and back six times a year. Her longest walk was to Greenock on the Clyde, then from there to Truro in Cornwall. She did this when trying to find some information about her husband's relatives. She was 92 years old at the time!

Being unsuccessful in her quest, she walked back from Truro to London, where the kindly Lord Mayor gave her the railway fare back to Sheffield.

SHEFFIELD'S OLDEST TREE

THERE MUST BE many old trees in the city's parks, but the most ancient must surely be the one situated in the Botanical Gardens. This is a fossilised bole and roots which was unearthed during mining for coal under Sheffield.

The tree stump was formerly in High Hazels Park, but has been moved to its present position to protect it from vandalism. It is estimated to be about 250,000,000 years old!

THE BOTANICAL GARDENS

THE BOTANICAL GARDENS were opened in 1836 on land purchased from the Wilson family of Sharrow. One of the most striking features of the gardens were the three large conservatories, linked by glass corridors, built to the design of B.B. Taylor, the Sheffield City Architect. Later the corridors were removed, leaving just the three large conservatories to house the beautiful and exotic plants brought from all over the world. One of the most impressive of these plants was a water lily, the Victoria Regia, which had rose-white flowers nearly two feet in diameter. The leaves of this plant were immense, being from six to twelve feet in diameter.

Two of the conservatories were converted in recent times into an aviary and an aquarium, but these have been shut down and now all three formerly beautiful glass buildings are in a sorry state!

One of the conservatories showing damage to the roof glass

THE MYTHICAL GODS OF SCOTLAND STREET

WHEN THE office building of Brass Founders Ltd was built in 1964, two finely sculptured bronze figures were placed on the front edge of the roof. On the left-hand side, facing the building, was an unknown figure holding a spear. This was created by a French sculptor, Antoine Coysevox, who lived from 1640 to 1720. On the right-hand side, there was a mythical Greek god playing a pipe (probably Pan), sculptured by Nicholas Coustou, a Frenchman who was born in 1658 and died in 1733.

Both figures were cast by F. Barbedienne and were exhibited at the great Paris Exhibition of 1862.

For many years the two Greek gods were in the possession of Mr H.C. Else and stood in his garden at Ford, near Ridgeway.

Unfortunately, owing to the increase in crime in Sheffield, especially the stealing of antiques (for instance, the loss of the beautiful Western Park gates and the urns from the Botanical Gardens), the two gods of Scotland Street have had to be taken down and removed to a safe place.

Pan, playing his pipe

♪HEFFIELD'S FIRST RAILWAY

IN THE YEAR 1836 an effort had been made to persuade the Midland Railway Company to lay a line to Sheffield, but without success. However, in October 1838, a railway was opened between Rotherham and Sheffield, the Sheffield station being situated at the bottom of Spital Hill. This line was named 'The Sheffield and Rotherham Railway' and was for some years our town's only contact with the Midland Railway. A local newspaper reported the opening of the line, on 31st October, in these words:

> *On that morning, about twenty minutes to eleven o'clock, the 'Victory' engine was heard to emit a loud whistle. This to my ears seemed a sort of scream, as though a bad accident had occurred. However, the train moved away carrying 300 passengers and amidst the shouts of many thousands of spectators, the speed gradually increased. The time for the first journey was 17 minutes. There was then a sumptuous breakfast at Rotherham, attended by all the notables of the district and George and Robert Stephenson. A dinner also took place at the Tontine Hotel at Sheffield. No charge was made that day, but afterwards the fares were: First Class One Shilling, Second Class Nine Pence, Third Class Six Pence.*

Odd Grave Markings

IN THE churchyard at Dore there are a few very small gravestones on which the only markings are 'S.P. FULL UP'.

These mark the spot of mass graves of mostly Irish navvies who died of smallpox (S.P.) in the late 19th century whilst constructing the Dore and Chinley Railway line.

Life was very cheap in those days!

Mass grave at Dore

DID SHE DIE OF A BROKEN HEART?

AN INSCRIPTION on a gravestone in Christ Churchyard, Attercliffe, reads:

> *In memory of Samuel Kitching. Died 3rd July, 1871, aged 58 years.*
> *Also Mary Wood Kitching, his wife. Died 13th July, 1871, aged 64 years.*

An epitaph also in the same churchyard reads:

> *Daniel Rowly—Died 30th April, 1879.*
>
> *A sudden change I in a moment felt,*
> *I had not time to bid my friends farewell.*
> *Think this not strange, Death happens unto all,*
> *This day was mine, tomorrow you may fall.*

A TERRIBLE MURDER

THOUGH MOST of the gravestones in the churchyard of St James have been moved and now lean against the walls, amongst the ones not too badly damaged can be seen a stone on which is the following inscription:

> *Sacred to the Memory of Charles, son of Charles and Hannah Glover of Holmhirst, who departed this life July 5th, 1846, aged 16 years.°*
>
> *In evil hour I fell*
> *Oppressed with pain,*
> *By bloody minded men*
> *Untimely slain.*

Obviously this poor lad was set upon by a gang of men and foully murdered!

A STANDING BURIAL

WHEN RESTORATIONS were made to the very ancient Church of St James at Norton, a memorial stone dated 1674, which lay under the altar adjoining the east window, was found to tell the unusual story of Barbara Lee. This lady was buried under the fireplace which was at that time situated on the site of the altar. The body was buried upright in a perpendicular hole, with the fireplace over the head. The reason for this was that there was so little room left for bodies under the church floor that there was no other way to lay the coffin.

 Tomb Music

IN THE CHURCHYARD of St George's, Portabello, is a most unusual tomb on which is carved the notes and words of a hymn.

> *Great God! What do I see and hear,*
> *The end of things created,*
> *The Judge of Mankind doth appear*
> *On clouds of glory seated.*

The person interred was Benjamin Coldwell who was the owner of the Nursery Lime and Plaster Works. He died in 1868, aged 82 years.

In 1855 Coldwell wrote a 'Handbook' in which he invited anyone interested to visit his library. There he had a wonderful collection of books, documents, drawings and plans. Amongst the latter were various elevations of St George's Church. There were also drawings of monuments, large houses and roads, mostly in Sheffield. Even his small handbook is a mine of information.

All the contents of his library could be studied for the small charge of sixpence!

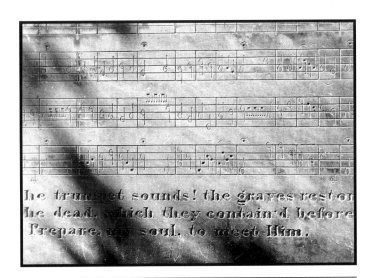

A Tudor Chip Shop

PITSMOOR was originally called 'Or-pits', the name meaning the pits from which ore was obtained. Except for these pits, the area was mostly agricultural or thick woodland. Practically all the last vestiges of Pitsmoor village have vanished, but it is still possible to see the Old Toll Bar House, standing at the junction of the Burngreave and Pitsmoor Roads. Abbeyfield House can still be seen in the park of the same name. However, lower down towards Burngreave, on Andover Street, there is a Tudor house of great interest. Originally called 'The White House', this was one of the widely scattered buildings of the area. Eventually in modern times the house became a chip shop, which must make it one of the very few Tudor Chip Shops in Britain!

HE MILK PARADE

THE SHEFFIELD Volunteer Yeomanry held parades which delighted the public in the nineteenth century. They had a variety of horses, many of them being used to pull milk carts during the week.

When parading through the town on Sundays, many youths would shout 'Milk', causing all the milk cart horses to stop! This caused great laughter amongst the spectators watching.

 BIG CONCESSION

AN EXTRACT from the Sheffield Evening Star for Thursday 24th May, 1883, read:

> *The action taken by the drapers on Sheffield Moor in closing their premises at five o'clock on Fridays, in order to allow their employees to have a few hours holiday each week, is worthy of imitation, not only by drapers, but by other tradesmen throughout the town.*

At that time the shop assistants had only Sunday for leisure. On Saturdays it was customary to work until 10 or 11 pm.

Unusual Gas Lamps

IN VARIOUS PARTS of Sheffield Mr Webb's Patent Sewer Gas Destructor Lamps can still be seen working more than one hundred years after he invented them.

In spite of their name, the lamps do not burn sewer gas—the light comes form ordinary gas, making hot air which draws the sewer fumes up through the column to burn off harmlessly.

The lamps were originally the property of the Yorkshire Water Authority, but were bought by the City Council in 1978.

Sewer Gas Destructor Lamp at junction of Westbourne Road and Ashdell Road, Broomhill

Boating at Moorfoot

IN THE EARLY nineteenth century, Eyre Street and Norfolk Street were the abode of doctors, clergymen and merchants. On Sheffield Moor, from the Moorhead to the old horse dyke at the foot, there were only two large houses, these belonging to Mr Holy and Mr Newbould. Near the foot of the Moor was the Woodman's Inn and a few cottages. Where Ellin Street is now was Green Bank House and grounds. Here resided Thomas Ellin, Master Cutler in 1841. All around were fields and trees, with a large stretch of water known as Bennett's Dam on which the local people boated!

Blood Suckers

WHEN WESTFIELD HOUSE on West Street became the Sheffield Dispensary in 1833, one of the constantly recurring accounts was for 'leech women'. In one year the number of leeches used in the Dispensary was 3,500 and they were all supplied by specialist leech women.

Accounts for the Dispensary would read, 'To Mrs Meadow's bill for applying leeches, £1:10:0. To Mrs Mellow's bill for applying leeches, £1:2:6.'

This practice of extracting blood by leeching was carried on until 1859, when it fell into disuse as a routine treatment. However, the author understands that leeches are still used occasionally at the Royal Hallamshire Hospital!

GOLDEN ATTERCLIFFE

NO PART of the city has changed more than Attercliffe. An old man who lived most of his life in that area, wrote the following in 1976.

If I could have my childhood days over again I would still choose Attercliffe to live in. My memories are golden!

We never heard the word vandalism and if we had, we would not have known what it meant. We had the most marvellous and kindest headmaster ever known and we all called him Daddy Vine. He was father to all and even the roughest boys respected him.

Our pleasures were queuing in Chapel Lane to see magic lantern shows at Attercliffe Wesleyan Hall on Sunday nights; with the Band of Hope on Monday, to let off steam; and singing 'My Drink is Water Bright' at the Salvation Army on Eadon Road.

We borrowed books from the library; held back-yard concerts, with all pals welcome; and there were the Scouts, Boy's Brigade, Guides and Sunday Schools, with their beautiful banners for the Whit Walk.

Attercliffe church bells rang Sunday morning and evening, and I learned to tell the time from Attercliffe Church clock. Then there was the Black and White Minstrel Jazz Band parade down Attercliffe Road on Easter Monday. Then on May Day, how beautiful the horses looked, all trimmed up with coloured braid and polished brasses.

But the finest thing was that everyone had real friends and good neighbours.

Note: 'Daddy Vine' was G.R. Vine, BSc., Headmaster of Huntsman's Gardens Council School, 1906–23. He wrote *The Story of Old Attercliffe*, published in 1936.

𝒜 FAMOUS SON OF ATTERCLIFFE

SIR ROBERT ABBOTT HADFIELD was born at Attercliffe on 28th November, 1858. He was the son of Robert Hadfield, who founded a firm for the making of steel castings. Working in his father's laboratory at the works, Robert eventually took out a patent for a tough, durable, non-magnetic manganese steel. In 1884 he conducted his first successful experiments with silicon steel, highly electrical and magnetic and of high tensile strength. Later he became world famous as a pioneer in the development of alloy steels. He was Master Cutler in 1899 and later had the honour of being made a Freeman of the City of Sheffield. Sir Robert died on 30th September, 1940.

The birthplace of Sir Robert Abbott Hadfield. The part building on the right is the Vestry Hall.

The Hill Top Chapel, Attercliffe

When the Hill Top chapel was built in 1629 it was much larger than we see it today. It was built mostly with the aid of Stephen and John Bright of Carbrook Hall and it is recorded that 'Mr Bright procured a bell and beautified the quire [choir] with sentences of scripture at his own charge.' The cost of building the chapel was £109 and the price of the land was £3.8s.0d. Two stonemasons, Thomas Arnalde and Henry Barber, were engaged to build the walls. The initials of these workmen, with the date 1629, can be seen carved in the stone over the small northern doorway. Thomas Hicks, a carpenter, then constructed the roofing and John Wilson was chosen to receive the people's free will offerings and to pay the workmen's wages.

In the nineteenth century the Chapel fell into disuse, so in 1897 the chapel was altered to its present size. However, it was not until 1909 that it was properly restored and rededicated for divine service. In the mid 1900s it again fell into ruin, but was restored again in July 1992 by the Sheffield Development Corporation and the City Council.

Hill Top Chapel in 1996

BENJAMIN HUNTSMAN, INVENTOR OF CRUCIBLE STEEL

NEARBY the Hill Top Chapel can be seen the restored grave of Benjamin Huntsman, a Doncaster clockmaker who came to live in Handsworth in 1740. In the course of his work Huntsman found the steel springs, which were then made with imported Swedish and German materials, unsatisfactory and he came to Sheffield to experiment with steel to find if he could produce springs of a more reliable nature. His experiments led to the invention of crucible steel. Huntsman built new works in Church Street, Attercliffe, he himself living in a house now called the Britannia Inn, which can still be seen on Worksop Road.

Benjamin Huntsman died on 29th June, 1776, aged 72 years.

The tomb of Huntsman in Hill Top Churchyard

A GRUESOME SIGHT

FROM 1752 an Act of Parliament gave judges the power to direct that the dead body of a thief or murderer could be hung in chains on a gibbet. The particularly gruesome method of doing this was that the chains were suspended from a hook in the beam of the gibbet in the form of a loop passing between the legs of the culprit where a curved piece of iron helped to support the body. An iron collar, fastened to the chain, was then riveted round the neck. Thus the body hung in chains, with the arms and legs dangling. Sometimes the body was covered in pitch and to prevent people climbing the gibbet post it was studded with innumerable nails.

In February 1971, Spence Broughton, once a wealthy Lincolnshire farmer, and his companion, John Oxley, held up the Sheffield and Rotherham Mail and stole the post bags. Both made good their escape and it was not until the following October that they were arrested in London. Oxley some-

how managed to escape from Clerkenwell Prison, but he also met a gruesome end, his body being found on Loxley Moor in February 1793. Spence Broughton was tried at York, found guilty and was executed in April 1792. On the following Monday morning his body, which had been brought back to Sheffield, was hung in chains on a gibbet on Attercliffe Common, near the scene of the robbery. This event created great public interest and for the next few days the road between Sheffield and Rotherham was crowded with a mass of people anxious to view the wretched spectacle of the body on the gibbet.

The bones of the mail robber hung there for 36 years, until they crumbled and dropped from the chains.

A new public house, The Noose and Gibbet Inn, was opened on Broughton Lane on 11th December 1995, outside of which is a gibbet and an effigy of Spence Broughton in a metal cage.

Attercliffe Common, 1792. On the left is the Arrow Inn; in the far centre is Carbrook Hall; on the right is the Old Pheasant Inn. On the extreme right the body of Spence Broughton hangs on the gibbet.

Effigy of
Spence
Broughton
in a
metal
cage

The Noose and
Gibbet Inn

THE NOOSE & GIBBET INN IS DEDICATED TO THE HIGHWAYMAN SPENCE BROUGHTON

— WHO WAS A GENTLEMAN FARMER
FROM LINCOLN.
HE MARRIED WELL, AND RECEIVED A
HANDSOME DOWRY. BUT THROUGH HIS LOVE
OF GAMBLING AT THE COCK FIGHTS, HE
SQUANDERED ALL. TO RECOUP HIS LOSSES,
HE TURNED TO CRIME, AND BECAME A
MEMBER OF THE HATTERS CLUB. A LOCAL
BAND OF ATTERCLIFFE VILLIANS. BUT HIS
LIFE OF CRIME WAS SHORT LIVED.
HE WAS HUNG IN THE YEAR OF OUR
LORD 1792 FOR THE ROBBERY OF THE
SHEFFIELD MAIL ON ATTERCLIFFE COMMON.

HE WAS HUNG AND GIBBETED
CLOSE TO THIS SPOT WHERE HIS REMAINS
WERE LEFT ON VIEW FOR SOME 37 YEARS
AS A DETERRENT TO OTHER WOULD BE
THIEVES AND BRIGANDS.
HE WAS THE LAST MAN TO BE SO
TREATED IN YORKSHIRE.
YOU WILL FIND INSIDE THIS FINE &
HOSPITABLE ESTABLISHMENT, ARTIFACTS
& WRITINGS RELATING TO THIS PERIOD
IN TIME.
SOME ARE FACT. SOME ARE FABLE.
& SOME OUTRIGHT BLARNEY.

Plaque in
front of the
Noose and
Gibbet Inn

Carbrook Hall, 1910

Carbrook Hall, 1996

𝒜 Climbing Musician

ONE OF THE odd characters of the town was William Battye, who was not only famous for the speeches he gave at the Cutlers Feast. One day he climbed the tower of the Parish Church (now the Cathedral) and when at the top of the steeple played a tune on his French horn!

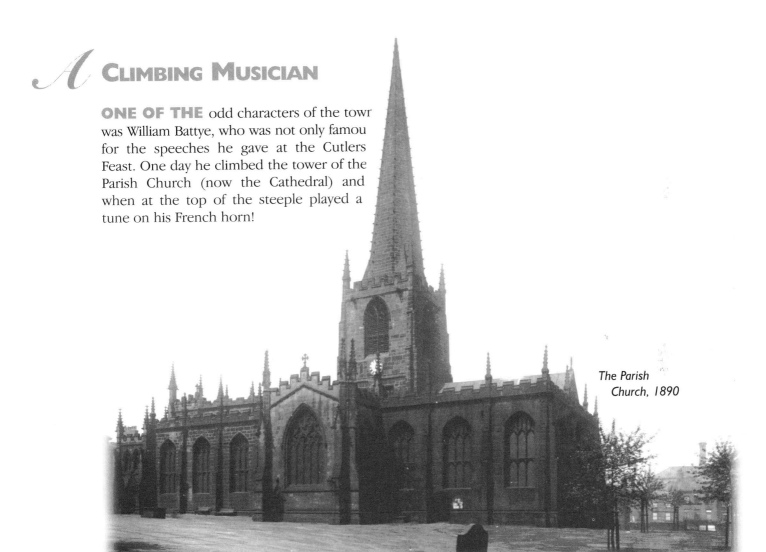

The Parish Church, 1890

HE DOG FIGHT

THE REVEREND Frank Parker of Dore was a remarkable character. One Sunday in the early 19th century, two dogs entered the church while he was preaching and began fighting. The parson refused to have them put out and leaning over the front of the pulpit, he exclaimed, 'Bet the black un'll win!'

OH THAT JAZZ!

SIR HENRY COWARD, a famous Sheffield musician and conductor, hated jazz.

At the Annual Dinner of the Abbeydale Orchestra in October, 1933, he made a strong outburst against modern jazz music.

'Jazz' exploded Sir Henry, 'has been responsible for destroying the prestige of the white race in the eyes of the nations. The natives see these people wallowing in the lascivious music which they themselves had used at their own riotous festivals. The natives then say, 'Ah, they are not better than we are!'

'Thus', said Sir Henry, 'no coloured race looks up to the Englishman in the way they used to. Jazz is one of the reasons for the disturbances in India, China, Japan and Africa. They do not regard the Englishman now in the same way they did twenty years ago. It has been this degrading jazz—the lewd dances and the frivolous air with which it is associated—that has brought about this deplorable state of affairs!'

If Sir Henry was alive today, one wonders how he would have got on with the Race Relations Act and what he would have said about modern rock music and the people that perform it!

HE EMPTY TOMB

A FEW YEARS AGO, behind the Cathedral, could be seen a finely decorated tomb. This was constructed for a member of the Shrewsbury family, but was never used. It formerly stood in the centre of the private Shrewsbury Chapel in the Cathedral (then the Parish Church), but when the Duke of Norfolk relinquished the Chapel in 1933, restoration work was begun and the empty tomb was moved to a position in the churchyard near Campo Lane. It was later dismantled when the Cathedral shop was installed and it was stated at the time that the restored tomb would be replaced somewhere in the church. However, there are no signs of this being carried out.

The Knock-Knobbler

IN THE EARLY 19th century the Parish Church (now the Cathedral) had a Peace Keeper, known to all and sundry as the 'Knock-Knobbler'. This position was held for many years by a man called 'Owd Bashford', who would sit on the lower step of the pulpit during the sermon, with a long bamboo cane across his knee. When anyone fell asleep, which was quite a common thing during the long and boring sermons, Owd Bashford would smartly tap them on the top of their heads with his cane. In other words, 'knock their nobs'.

The Peace Keeper also had a whip which he used on any stray dogs entering the church.

He would also go with the Church 'Mesters' on their visits, during the service, to the neighbouring public houses to see that no drunkenness or gambling was going on. If any person was caught playing 'chuck farthing' or 'shuffle board', he would be taken out and fastened in the town stocks which stood near the church gates. There the victim was left exposed to the jeers and insults of the passers-by.

A FAMOUS SHEFFIELD THEATRE

ON MONDAY November 4th, 1895, a new theatre, the Empire Palace of Varieties, opened in Charles Street. Designed by Frank Matcham and built by Longdens of Sheffield, no expense was spared to make the theatre outwardly and inwardly worthy, in every way, of the city.

Frank Allen, general manager of Moss & Thornton's Provincial Empires Ltd, came to Sheffield to supervise the opening, and he announced that the forthcoming attractions would include such giants of the music hall as Little Tich, Dan Leno and Vesta Tilley.

Despite the competition from the new Empire (all 3,500 seats were filled), the other theatres in Sheffield had full houses on opening night. 'The Trumpet Call' was at the Alexandra; 'A Knight in Armour' at the City Theatre; and the 'Notorious Mrs Ebbsmith' at the Theatre Royal. Those who did not want drama could see Mrs Alice Harvey, the mimic, at the Grand Theatre of Varieties; while opening at the Edmund Road Drill Hall was the Tussaud's Exhibition, direct from London.

However, the Empire, which closed nearly 40 years ago, eventually took a lot of the custom away from the other theatres in Sheffield, and was partly responsible for the demise of the West Bar area as an entertainment centre.

Miss Vesta Tilley

Miss Vesta Tilley in Male Dress

STATE SERIES   MISS VESTA TILLEY.   1512

PHILCO SERIES 6002 B   VESTA TILLEY.   THE DRAYCOTT GALLERIE

Miss Gertie Millar

Miss Ethel Oliver

11. Miss Gertie Millar.

ETHEL OLIVER.

TROUBLE AT THE SHEFFIELD THEATRES

IN 1910 a French music hall comedienne ran into censorship trouble at the Empire Theatre. It appears she changed her costume in full view of the audience several times and one of her songs reached the 'limit of suggestiveness'. Complaints were made to the Chief Constable that the comedienne, Mlle Liant D'Eve was guilty of gross indecency, and the chief warned the theatre management that action would be taken if the act was not changed. Both houses were packed on the second night, but by then the act had been greatly modified. One song had been dropped, the girl changed her clothes in the wings, and some of the gestures she had used the previous night had been taken out, all to the disgust of the menfolk in the audience!

The auditorium of the Empire Theatre

The Lyceum Theatre

A BUILDING of which most Sheffielder's are very proud is the Lyceum Theatre in Tudor Square. It was opened in 1897, the architect being W.G.R. Sprague. At the beginning of 1972 it became obvious to many people that, unless something was done to preserve it, the theatre was doomed! In November of that year the Hallamshire Historic Buildings Society had managed to get 'listed' many buildings in the Surrey/Norfolk Street area, the Lyceum amongst them. This meant that before the theatre could be demolished a public inquiry would have to be held. In December one of the Labour councillors launched a scathing attack on conservationists for having persuaded the Government to preserve the now closed theatre. 'I call these people vultures,' he said. 'They sit in their eyries, look down and see what they want to preserve and then swoop down and get it!'

The amusing thing is that, almost opposite this beautiful renovated theatre, on the wall of a building at the top of Howard Street, is a fine representation of four vultures. These are now known, unofficially, as the 'Listing Committee' of the Hallamshire Historic Buildings Society!

The four vultures

The Lyceum Theatre in 1996

The Moving Stocks

The Wadsley Jack

BECAUSE OF traffic problems in the 1970s, stocks which had stood for over a hundred years near the Star Inn, at the junction of Rural Lane and Laird Road, were moved to the grass verge at the top of Rydalhurst Avenue.

In 1976, the inn, run by the landlord, Mr James Pulfrey, was renamed 'The Wadsley Jack', after a cutler who lived and worked in the village. During the following year, the stocks were replaced near to their original site close to the public house.

The ancient stocks

No Wonder the Hospital Beds Were Full!

WHEN THE Public Hospital (later to become the Royal Hospital on West Street) had its accounts checked by the Finance Committee, there came to light some rather unusual items of undue expenditure.

The Committee found that from January to June, 1871, there had been consumed at the hospital: 27 gallons of ale, 252 gallons of bitter beer and 1,392 bottles of port!

The Odd Streaker

IN THE mid-nineteenth century, on a busy afternoon, a pretty young woman, completely naked, rushed out of a passage near Lady's Bridge and dodging the horses and carts that thronged the area, crossed over the Wicker to the other side.

As can be imagined, people just stopped and stared in amazement and one carter fell from his dray as his horse reared up as the woman ran past.

Eventually the young lady disappeared from sight down another passage at the side of a public house, but the crowds waited, expecting some irate man to appear chasing after her. However, much to their disgust, nothing happened and after a time the people moved on about their business.

Though a number of newspaper reporters tried to discover the identity of the woman, they were unsuccessful and the whole incident remains a mystery to this day!

$\mathcal{J}$HEFFIELD'S MODERN SCULPTURES

IN MAY 1972, a giant red steel sculpture was erected near the Crucible Theatre. This 20-foot-high arch, a tribute to Sheffield's industrial heritage, was the work of Bernard Schottlander. Nearby, just outside the Polytechnic (now the Hallam University) in Arundel Gate, was a second sculpture (known as the 'Pack of Cards') by Sheffield-born Kenneth Martin. Both these sculptures were on loan for six months, after which they could be purchased by the Sheffield Council or returned to the Peter Stuyvesant Foundation.

Neither of the sculptures were liked by the Sheffield public: in fact they became a standing joke, so both were eventually returned to the Foundation.

Another unusual sculpture was erected outside the Sheffield Children's Hospital in 1977. This was a 15-foot-high collection of twisted tubes by William Pye which cost £5,000. When asked by the press what it was called, Pye said, 'I have not yet given it a name, but I shall when I've had a good think about how the sculpture looks!' The press had many letters, mostly critical and 48 members of the Medical Records Department of the Children's Hospital wrote saying how much they all disliked the sculpture.

In May 1978, an unusual Horse and Rider sculpture was erected in Barker's Pool, on the Foundation Precinct site. This interesting work of art by David Wynne is 12 feet high and weighs about a ton. It was commissioned jointly by a London Financial Advisor, Jonathan Stone, Chairman of Brook Shaws, the Sheffield Motor Company, and by Slough Estates Ltd, which owns the Fountain Precinct. Mr Stone wanted the sculpture as a memorial to his father, Hyman Stone, a Sheffield solicitor, whose office was once on the corner of Barker's Pool and Fargate.

At the rear of the Manpower Services' huge building at the Moorfoot is an Abstract Water Sculpture set in a hexagonal pool. This work was by the Yorkshire sculptor Judith Bluck and cost £30,000. It is a feature based on a local theme—the Crucible—and is made of steel and bronze. It was erected in 1981.

In 1983 a life-size statue of 'Simple Walking Man' was placed outside the modern Town Hall extensions. It is the work of the late George Fullard, a local sculptor. Further examples of Fullard's work can be seen in the graveyard to the front of Upper Chapel in Norfolk Street.

Sculpture, Children's Hospital

Abstract water sculpture

Horse
and Rider

The-**Unseen** *the* **Unsightly** *and the* **Amusing** *in* **Sheffield**

*Woman
and Child*

Simple Walking Man

The–**Unseen** the **Unsightly** and the **Amusing** in **Sheffield**

The-Unseen the Unsightly and the Amusing in Sheffield

IMAGES OF SHEFFIELD'S industrial past were revived on 13th August 1991, when a giant stainless steel sundial was erected in the East End. The sundial was created by the sculptor Wendy Taylor, and was commissioned to commemorate Harry Brearley, the Sheffield inventor of stainless steel. It is positioned on the site of the former Brown Bayley steelworks where Mr Brearley was works manager and technical director at the turn of the century. The cost of the modern sculpture was £40,000.

An abstract sculpture that caused quite a lot of controversy and not a little amusement is the one near the Wicker Arches. This 22-foot-high stainless steel work was created by Amanda King and was erected opposite the arches at the junction of Spital Hill and Saville Street in 1993. Many letters to the press criticised the sculpture and one man offered to give a similar work from his scrap yard absolutely free!

Not really a sculpture, but a huge cast steel component used to build offshore oil and gas rigs, now stands on the roundabout at the junction of Brightside Lane and Upwell Street. The component was donated by the Sheffield firm River Don Castings which stands nearby.

The River Don Works was originally Vickers & Sons, and on the preserved main building it is still possible to see the 'V' for Vickers above all the windows.

Now on display in the Lower Don Valley is a huge industrial steam hammer, formerly to be seen at Kelham Museum. This 25-foot-high machine was constructed by the Brightside Engineering Company and used by the nearby Firth Brown Atlas works. It is now situated on the island at the junction of Saville Street East and Sutherland Street.

Industrial steam hammer

The Vickers building

A huge cast steel component

THE AMUSING
—BUT TRUE

A Traveller's View of Sheffield in 1797

MR J. GRANT, ESQ., was a great traveller around Britain. These were his views on Sheffield when he visited the town in 1797.

Its streets are ill paved, its inns dear and dirty, its neighbourhood adorned with men hanging in chains. It fact, it is one of the most smoky ugly towns I have ever travelled through or rested in. It is however, rich and commercial.

A King's Opinion

ABOUT THE YEAR 1800, the children of Mr Shore, of Norton Hall, were on the beach at Weymouth under the care of a nurse. Weymouth was at that time the favourite resort of His Majesty George III, and one day, whilst the children were playing, the King walked by. With good-natured inquisitiveness the King inquired whose children they were. When the nurse, with a curtsey, replied, 'May it please your Majesty, they are Mr Shore's of Norton, near Sheffield,' King George said, 'Ah, Sheffield, Sheffield. Damned bad place, Sheffield!'

Thank Goodness for Our Golden Frame!

KING GEORGE'S view seemed to have been shared by Horace Walpole, who after visiting the town described Sheffield as 'One of the foulest towns in England, in the most charming situation!'

*The-**Unseen** the **Unsightly** and the **Amusing** in **Sheffield***

A Reporter's View of Sheffield

JOHN FOSTER FRASER, a reporter on a weekly newspaper, came to Sheffield during the nineteenth century. He styled the town as 'A suburb of Hell!' He also said:

> *In one respect Sheffield is like Frankenstein, it has created a monster and is proud of it, and all the world looks and applauds. But Sheffield should remember that it is the monster which makes men undersized and crooked limbed, and gives them cheeks which are ashen. Sheffield is a city of the physically damned!*

A Bishop's View

THE BISHOP of London, Dr Ingram, visited Sheffield in June 1921. He told a large gathering that, since the war, drunkenness had increased by 106 per cent. He pleaded for the Sunday closing of houses, restricted drinking hours, fewer licences, abolition of grocer's licences, no sale of liquor to young people, increased powers for magistrates and control of clubs.

Sheffield in 1899

SIR CHARLES DILKE, speaking at the Albert Hall in October, 1899 said:

> *Sheffield may be regarded as one of Ruskin's cities, clotted and coagulated with spots of a dreadful mildew, full of those to whom the cradle is a curse. It contains houses unrepaired because they have been condemned, yet inhabited because there are no others.*

A Canadian Opinion

A MR J.A. MACDONALD, writing in the *Toronto Globe*, after a visit to Sheffield in 1909, said the following:

> *I have before today looked out into the green meadows that surround this cosmic accident called Sheffield. Although I don't believe Sheffield is much worse than most places, your horror, your squalor, your misery, has a knack of coming out on to the street more than in any other town!*

An Aerodrome is a Must!

WHEN SIR ALAN COBHAM, the pioneer aviator, came to Sheffield in May 1929, he said:

Trade follows the aeroplane and aviation means trade to Sheffield. I want to make the Corporation realise this. If they don't, the next generation will rain their curses on them.

The town that does not have its own aerodrome will soon be left out of it in the future. Sheffield must have its flying base. Not until every town has its aerodrome and we can fly from town to town with ease, will aviation be a success in this country!'

Praise for Sheffield

THE RIGHT REVEREND Leonard Hedley Burrows, speaking of his 25 years as Bishop of Sheffield, in 1939, said 'The longer I live, the more thankful I am that I came to Sheffield!'

Our Poor Railway Service

MR BRIAN HINCHCLIFFE, railway expert, stated in August 1969:

Sheffield must be quite the most atrociously served city in the country, with railway services in every direction worse now than in almost any other peace time year of the present century.

Dr Edith Summerskill MP on Sheffield's Clean Air

INAUGURATING Sheffield's clean-air campaign in November, 1959, Dr Edith Summerskill said:

This morning I drove around Sheffield looking for black smoke. I only found one wisp! Sheffield is in the forefront of the fight for clean air and is translating into action the Act of Parliament that deals with it.

Satisfied Householders

THE DEPARTMENT of the Environment announced in April, 1979

More than 80 per cent of the 199,000 households in Sheffield are satisfied, or very satisfied, with the area they live in!

Buildings Are of No Importance!

IN 1969 Mr Peter Shepheard, president of the Royal Institute of British Architects, opened an exhibition in Sheffield. His most amazing statement was:

In the past architects had been much too interested in the beauty of their buildings without realising that what mattered to everybody was all the buildings and the spaces in between. In fact, if you give me the spaces in between, I don't really care so much what the buildings look like!

Not For Us —A Press Report

IN THE MINUTES of the Sheffield City Council Town Planning Committee's last meeting (1971), the Environment Sub-committee reports on an invitation to the city to enter a Conservation Awards Scheme, sponsored by the Royal Institution of Chartered Surveyors and the *Times*.

The Estates Surveyor and the City Planning Officer and Architect both considered the invitation—but neither could think of a suitable entry from the Corporation.

No comment!

*Snig Hill 1880,
showing Tudor
buildings on left*

*The-**Unseen** the **Unsightly** and the **Amusing** in **Sheffield***

THE CURSE OF DEVELOPERS

THE FOLLOWING is an extract from a letter sent to the Yorkshire Post in June 1973.

Why is it that as soon as an area in the condition that God made it comes to notice, some oafish Philistine want to step in and develop it? The seeds of this kind of destruction are sown by self-styled environmentalists who can find no delight in a stretch of water unless power boats are screaming across it, to whom empty fields are an abomination lacking duly planned caravan sites with leisure centre attached, in whose eyes open moorland can be vastly improved by the construction of golf courses and sports complexes.

The seeds are watered by local authorities and regional development councils anxious to justify their existence by seeking to appear progressive. Fertilised by hard cash they yield a rich reward to the developers.

Thus another once-quiet corner of England is ulcerated to the joy of the planners—the cry of birds, the music of wind in the reeds, the soft, quiet of calm water all subjected to a concrete and plastic order where transistorised man can enjoy the good life at the touch of a button!

WHY THE GUNS DID NOT FIRE

DURING THE First World War, the Germans used Zeppelins to bomb English cities. Sheffield was raided on the night of Monday, 25th September, 1916 and much damage was caused by the bombs.

Although there were batteries of guns and searchlights at the Manor, Wincobank Hill and Ecclesall, not one shot was fired. It appears that all the officers and the gun crews were at the Grand Hotel, entertaining a pilot who had shot down a Zeppelin over Cuffley!

How Wrong Can You Be?

IN 1938, with the Second World War approaching rapidly, there were many debates about air-raid precautions in the Town Hall Council Chamber.

At a meeting a councillor stated that he was taking no interest whatsoever in air-raid precautions, except to advise people to have nothing to do with them. He went on to say, 'I do not believe a hostile aeroplane will ever arrive over Sheffield, for evidence proves conclusively that bombers can only go short distances and cannot possibly bomb our city!'

What the same councillor said after the nights of 12th and 15th December, 1940, are not recorded!

 LUCKY BOY

SHEFFIELD'S first juvenile court, set up to deal with children under 16, was officially opened by the Lord Mayor, Councillor Herbert Hughes, in October 1906.

A small boy, in a state of nervous terror at the magnitude of his offence, appeared accused of selling newspapers without permission at the Midland Station. He was told that since he had the honour of being the first child to appear before the court he would be let off!

Those who followed him were less fortunate. One was sent to a reformatory until he was 19 and another was sent down for six strokes of the birch!

 CITY HALL LIONS

WHEN OUR VERY FINE City Hall was built in 1934, the architect, E. Vincent Harris, had two stone Assyrian lions gracing either side of the large platform. These were criticised by certain people and especially Sir Henry Wood, the famous conductor. When the lions were discussed by the City Council in September 1936, one councillor said they looked fine from the back of the hall. 'From five or six miles away they would look even finer!' said another councillor. When a vote was taken it was decided the lions would stay and this they did for another 30 years.

Eventually they were bought by a Matlock firm and they can still be seen gracing the doorway of a building on the right-hand side of the Matlock to Matlock Bath road.

 HE HIGHFIELD COFFEE HOUSE

IN 1908 the oldest Coffee House in Sheffield closed down. Started in 1877 by Sir Frederick Mappin and his friends, it closed because the premises were too large for the requirements of the district. The premises of Barlows, shop fitters, now occupy the site.

The Bare Facts

IN JULY 1903, the Sheffield Education Committee agreed that nude models could be employed at the College of Art in Arundel Street.

However, the Lord Mayor moved an amendment, expressing doubt whether the study of the nude figure in art was favourable to the moral character. Only three members shared his doubt, so the amendment was lost.

The Mikado Banned!

SHEFFIELD received much publicity in May 1907 for giving a performance of Gilbert and Sullivan's 'The Mikado' at the Lyceum Theatre.

Somebody in authority had decided that the comic opera was undesirable because it might offend the Japanese and harm Anglo-Japanese relations at a time when Prince Fushimi was about to visit Britain. So its licence was withdrawn by the Lord Chamberlain.

Amateur companies throughout the country dropped their plans for performing the opera, but the D'Oyly Carte company said they had not been notified of the licence being withdrawn and they went ahead with their performance at the Lyceum.

There was talk of a possible prosecution, but it came to nothing and the opera, the D'Oyly Carte and Sheffield survived!

Mixed Bathing

EVEN AS LATE AS 1929, mixed bathing was not universally approved and when the Millhouses Bathing Pool was opened in that year there were some strict regulations. First the pool was divided in half lengthways: ladies and girls had the use of one half whilst the men and boys had the other. Wire netting was placed across the pool surrounds to divide the sexes. If a man or a woman swam across to the wrong side they were not allowed to rest their arms on the pool side but had to swim back again. To prevent people in the park from watching them, a huge hedge was planted at the public side of the pool. Eventually the Parks Committee realised how stupid these regulations were, the wire netting was removed and the sexes were allowed to mix.

Poor Workhouse Children

IT IS A SAD FACT that many of Sheffield's children had a hard life in the 19th century.

On the 28th January, 1885, at a meeting of the Sheffield Board of Guardians, it was stated that an invitation had been given for the Workhouse children to visit the pantomime at the Alexandra Theatre. Eight of the Guardians voted for the invitation to be accepted, with six voting against.

Another similar invitation was given to the children by the manager of the Theatre Royal on 4th February, but this was declined by the Guardians who replied, 'It is not considered advisable for the children to witness two pantomimes in one week!'

The Owls in Trouble

ON 27TH JANUARY, 1906, it was published in the press that a crowd of Sheffield supporters had attacked the Preston North End team as they left the ground, throwing stones, sticks and mud and spitting on the Preston players.

When the F.A. Commission inquired into the incident they concluded that the match was not played in the proper spirit, was not properly controlled by the referee, that the Preston director conducted himself improperly towards spectators and that Preston players conducted themselves in a vulgar manner at the dressing room windows. The Commission censured all players of both teams, the referee and both linesmen, fined all the Preston players one pound each and suspended the director from football management for a month.

Because of the crowd's behaviour, they closed the Wednesday ground for 14 days in February.

The Duke of Darnall

HARRY TAYLOR, better known as 'The Duke of Darnall' was born around the turn of the century. As a young man he worked as a core-maker at Brown Bailey's Steel Works. He was deaf and dumb, but could make odd noises and as he grew older he became extremely eccentric.

He first lived in Britannia Road, but later moved to Darnall Road where he lived in the centre cottage of three, which were situated just above the Ball Inn. For a time he lived with a well-known prostitute known locally as 'Russian Edna'. This lady of ill-repute was murdered in 1953. Harry Taylor denied any responsibility, writing on a piece of paper, 'I did not do it!' Shortly afterwards another man was charged with the murder, found guilty and sentenced to life imprisonment.

The Duke of Darnall dressed very smartly in a tailored suit, bowler hat, spats, polished shoes and always had a flower in his lapel. The clothes were provided for him by Burton's, the shoes by Langton's and the flowers by Artindales.

Most older people can remember the 'Duke' as he walked around the city centre. Harry would doff his hat to every lady and the only time he caused trouble was when he would stand in the middle of the road and direct traffic! All the policemen knew him and would gently lead him back onto the footpath.

The Duke of Darnall died around 1970, a great loss to Sheffield for we have now none of the odd characters that used to make life so much more interesting.

The Cremorne Gardens

MANY PEOPLE must be puzzled by the odd name of the public house on the corner of London Road and Alderson Road at Highfield.

The name came about when Henry Warhurst, who had formerly owned the Newhall Pleasure Gardens, left there and acquired the large mansion known as Mount Pleasant, which stands at the lower end of Sharrow Lane. Mr War-hurst then opened the grounds of Mount Pleasant to the public, calling them the Cremorne Gardens.

THE DANGEROUS TRAMCARS

NINE INQUESTS were held in the Coroner's Court on 20th January, 1920. Four were into the deaths of people who had been knocked down and killed by tramcars. A doctor from the Royal Infirmary said the cause was negligence and the trams were being driven too fast!

NOTHING EVER ALTERS!

ALSO IN 1920 a Corporation spokesman said that because of a shortage of mantles and burners, of 12,500 street lamps in Sheffield, only 7,000 were lit and it was thought that this was the cause of many accidents.

THE ICE CREAM KIOSK

ONE OF THE CITY'S great attractions in the year 1931 was a new traffic control system in the Town Hall Square. This incorporated flashing coloured lights and signals, rather like those used on the railway, controlled by policemen from a kiosk in the centre of the square.

Inside his glass box the policeman was surrounded by mirrors so that he could see all the traffic coming from any direction. When he saw a large queue waiting to cross the square (probably three cars and a bus!), he would pull a little lever and the appropriate signal would bob up and down and the lights would flash to allow the traffic to flow across the square.

In the early hours of May 21st, a group of young men dumped empty beer bottles in the kiosk and painted the words 'Ice Cream' on the outside of the glass box. Before the young men got away the flying squad appeared and 14 had their names taken!

There is no record of their punishment.

THE TOWN HALL EXTENSIONS AND BUCKINGHAM PALACE

IN FEBRUARY 1977, the Conservative leader on the Sheffield council said, 'The new Town Hall extensions (then being built on the site of St Paul's Church, now the Peace Gardens) will enjoy standards of luxury that will make Buckingham Palace look shoddy!'

Unfortunately the three-storey building, which cost over £11 million to build and fit out, has not been a success and is due to be demolished within the next year or so.

ART OR PLAIN RUBBISH?

AT THE BEGINNING OF 1981 there was an exhibition of modern art at the Mappin Art Gallery. This consisted of piles of stones, rubbish, leaves and earth and various other odds and ends. One of the art critics described the exhibition as 'Hard won simplicity, activating space, plus subtlety of the ordinary'.

However, the public was not impressed. 'It is a great confidence trick, this so-called modern art!' said one. 'The average person knows that much of the contemporary art scene is a vast sham and this includes the sculptures of Henry Moore and Barbara Hepworth who make a mint with the holes!'

Another visitor said, 'I am wondering who is the biggest nutcase, the exhibitor, the writer of the exhibition brochure, or the taxpayers who pick up the £15,000 bill!'

A NUDE IS NEWS

A PENCIL SKETCH called 'Standing Nude' by the famous artist and sculptor Eric Gill, was banned in Sheffield. The sketch showed a female torso, and it was part of the Sheffield Society of Artists' annual exhibition at the Mappin Art Gallery in 1931.

Councillor A. Barton, chairman of the Mappin Gallery Committee, said the committee was not squeamish and had no objection to ordinary nudes, but did not think that this one was suitable for public exhibition. He had never seen anything like it in any other gallery.

The sketch was withdrawn shortly before the exhibition opened!

The Unseen the Unsightly and the Amusing in Sheffield

THE RAPE OF CHANTREYLAND

IN 1981 a plaque was unveiled on the birthplace of Sir Francis Chantrey at Norton. The irony of this was that here were people giving homage to not only a great sculptor, but to a man who loved beauty, and, above all, his beloved Norton. Meanwhile, around his birthplace men and earth movers were creating havoc building a new road through some of the finest scenery in Sheffield.

Within a few yards of Chantrey's cottage they were tearing up the paddock in front of Jordanthorpe Hall. In addition the little Jordanthorpe Lodge was having most of its garden stripped away.

Just above, at Jordanthorpe Hall Farm, the historic cruck barn was just a pile of rubble, while, worst of all, the beautiful grounds of Oakes Park were having their age-old oaks torn up to make way for this violation.

Meanwhile, in the Civic newspaper the City Council were asking people to tell them how to combat vandalism!

Chantrey's cottage

WOULD IT BE THE END OF THE WORLD?

MANY PEOPLE believed that the experiments into the release of atomic energy which were being carried out at the Sheffield University in 1924 could result in the destruction of the world.

The man who was doing the experiment, Dr T.F. Wall, of the University's Applied Science department, received hundreds of letters from all over the country, asking him to stop.

Dr Wall said all precautions would be taken and if anything alarming happened he would cease and think the matter over.

The next day Dr Wall broadcast to the country from Sheffield Relay Station to explain what he was doing. It is estimated he had at least two million listeners. The scientist told them that any danger there might be in the experiment would be confined to the investigator himself.

The assurance seemed to pacify the people and afterwards the publicity died away.

*Our last
police box*

Information plaque

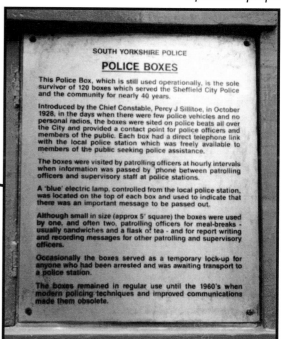

SOUTH YORKSHIRE POLICE

POLICE BOXES

This Police Box, which is still used operationally, is the sole survivor of 120 boxes which served the Sheffield City Police and the community for nearly 40 years.

Introduced by the Chief Constable, Percy J Sillitoe, in October 1928, in the days when there were few police vehicles and no personal radios, the boxes were sited on police beats all over the City and provided a contact point for police officers and members of the public. Each box had a direct telephone link with the local police station which was freely available to members of the public seeking police assistance.

The boxes were visited by patrolling officers at hourly intervals when information was passed by 'phone between patrolling officers and supervisory staff at police stations.

A 'blue' electric lamp, controlled from the local police station, was located on the top of each box and used to indicate that there was an important message to be passed out.

Although small in size (approx 5' square) the boxes were used by one, and often two, patrolling officers for meal-breaks - usually sandwiches and a flask of tea - and for report writing and recording messages for other patrolling and supervisory officers.

Occasionally the boxes served as a temporary lock-up for anyone who had been arrested and was awaiting transport to a police station.

The boxes remained in regular use until the 1960's when modern policing techniques and improved communications made them obsolete.

The–Unseen the Unsightly and the Amusing in Sheffield

OUR LAST REMAINING POLICE BOX

POLICE BOXES were introduced by the Chief Constable, Percy J. Sillitoe, in October 1928. There were 120 boxes and they were sited on police beats all over the city. They provided a contact point for police officers, each box having a direct telephone link with the local police station and the telephones could be used by the general public if they wished to call for assistance.

A blue electric lamp, controlled by the local police station, was located on top of each box and it indicated when lit that there was a message awaiting the nearest police officer.

The boxes remained in regular use until the 1960s, when modern policing techniques and improved communications made them obsolete.

The police box pictured opposite, which is situated on Surrey Street, at the corner of the Town Hall, is the last in Sheffield.

A QUEER BUILDING

ORIGINALLY CALLED 'The New Odeon Building', which took the site of the Gaumont Cinema in Barker's Pool, this row of shops and cinema caused much controversy and quite a lot of amusement. The usual question was, 'Why have they left the scaffolding in place and then painted it red?'

What is certain is that the building is not in keeping with any of the others in Barker's Pool!

𝒜 STATUE OF HERMES

OVER THE ENTRANCE to the Bradford and Bingley building in High Street is the statue of Hermes. He was the son of Zeus who took him to be his messenger and ambassador. He later became the god of eloquence and good fortune, and the patron of merchants and travellers. Hermes wears the *petasus*, or broad-brimmed hat, bears the *caduceus*, or staff, and has winged sandals. The Romans also had this god but called him Mercury. The statue was originally placed on the building when it was Kemsley House, the home of the *Sheffield Independent* and the *Telegraph and Star*.

Front of the Festival of Britain Conservatory showing the tree growing through the roof in 1996

*The-**Unseen** the **Unsightly** and the **Amusing** in **Sheffield***

A Festival of Britain Disgrace

IN WESTON PARK, once one of our finest open spaces, situated next to the Sheffield University, there are the remains of a conservatory. This was built and opened in 1951 during the Festival of Britain. Full of exotic flowers, trees and water plants, it was a great attraction, not only to the Sheffield people, but to the many visitors to the city.

Unfortunately, like most of the city's parks and open spaces, Weston has been neglected, even though one of our finest buildings, the Mappin Art Gallery, is situated there.

The Festival Conservatory is in a shocking state; all the flowers are gone and a large eucalyptus tree has pushed its way through the roof.

As the chairman of the National Heritage Memorial Fund, Lord Rothschild, said recently, 'Many city parks are presently underfunded and undervalued and have become little more than litter-strewn, dog-fouled wildernesses.'

Perhaps one day Sheffield will become once again 'The City of Flowers'.

Side view of the Conservatory

*I*n Conclusion

A few of the curious objects to be seen in the centre of Sheffield.

Stone carving of a cat in
the Barker's Pool Gardens

Stone carvings of undistinguishable
animals in Castle Square

Winged lion
on pillar in
Castle Square

One of the
ugly lamp
standards
in Fargate

Strange stone
objects in the
centre of
High Street

INDEX

Alice looked at the objects wearily, 'Are you animal—or vegetable—or mineral?' she said, yawning at every other word.

With further apologies to Lewis Carroll